THE ECONOMY OF
WASTE

WITH COLLABORATION WITH
AILIN E. BABAKHANIAN AND EDWARD BABAKHANIAN

OKSEN BABAKHANIAN

authorHOUSE

AuthorHouse™
1663 Liberty Drive
Bloomington, IN 47403
www.authorhouse.com
Phone: 833-262-8899

Published by AuthorHouse   03/08/2021

ISBN: 978-1-6655-1891-8 (sc)
ISBN: 978-1-6655-1889-5 (hc)
ISBN: 978-1-6655-1890-1 (e)

Library of Congress Control Number: 2021904621

Print information available on the last page.

CONTENTS

PART III: HEALTCARE

PART IV: SYSTEMS

PART V: POLITICES

THE ECONOMY OF WASTE

1. Supply = Demand …. Not Really!
2. Supply = Demand + Credit + Waste

   If supply increases, there is a proportional rise in economy and thus a decrease in unemployment.
3. Demand = Needs…. Not Really!
4. Demand = Needs + Wants + Credit + Waste
5. Savings = Stagnation
6. Savings = Supply − Demand

   Saving decrease the supply and increase the demand.

PROPHASE

Supply is not only related to demand but also it has a strong linkage with waste factor. Let us define the waste factor. Waste factor is essentially destroying the planet especially when people buy things, they want but, do not actually need them. Although, waste is not entirely a negative phenomenon when we are discussing consumerism and business for entrepreneurs, but to create waste in a way to accomplish this which is as a strong and valuable point of the demand factor for supplies. They come up with two huge and innovative strategies.

The demand alone will not be sufficient to sustain a growing and robust economy. Since demand historically is a need drive factor, it is what people need to buy for their daily living and family sustainable is nothing extravagant. It is a humble request for things and items for a minimum or at most a medium living standard. That is the reason why most of countries in the world are poor or barely surviving. The demand put up by people in those countries is exceptionally low, it is for survival only. Another devastating factor on top of low demand is that the families, the core of the working and demanding society are always pushed and encouraged to save their mere earnings for "The rainy days". Therefore, again part of the available fund for investment has put in the safe box or moved out of circulation for savings, reducing further the demand for new goods and luxuries. This theory makes the countries poor and poorer. Because there is exceptionally low demand and exceptionally low waste, not many supplies are needed to meet the demand and waste factor.

Supply = Demand + Credit + Waste

Demand = Needs + Wants + Credit + Waste

Savings = Supply – Demand

Why waste?! It is a powerful enticement for the hungry and needy to dream big, to have items of his wishes and feel good about all the luxury items which only the rich can enjoy. Wow!

Can you imagine in a society that the poor and rich can afford the same luxury items?!

A poor person can sleep in the best hotels that only kings can afford. He can drive cars of his dreams, same way of the richest person in his life, having luxury home, boat, a lavish living, vacation etc.

Now, how can this happen? how a poor society with a low demand can transfer to high rolling, rich acting, spending society...

This can happen, only with two, or three brilliant ways:

I.   Marketing

II. Credit

III. Taxes

I. What is marketing? It is a professional way of selling items to people without consideration of their needs but use their greed and wishes. A good marketing agent can sell you the "The snake oil' to the highest bidder for pride of owning special boots, clothing and every size machine and diet pills. Each one of those sale figures is in billion yet, in poor society they do not have the slightest notion of these types of sale and marketing.

II. Credit: what is credit? It is money loaned to someone with an interest (which is compounded not a simple interest). No wonder Einstein said that nothing is as powerful as compounding interest.

Large credit companies have long discovered that the most people are honest and will pay their loan with a small payment if given the chance. Therefore, they give credit to lots of people, whether poor, rich, or working middle class with little work history charging a %20 or more compound interest with a low monthly payment, which usually will cover the interest portion only. By doing this, these companies create a huge pool of people demanding credit while being at %80 or more responsible for their payment for the portion of huge interest. Money allocated is so much that it will pay for the ones that do not pay or abuse the system.

Therefore, with credit in their pocket in the form of credit card with truly little sophistication, people are apt to pay attention to their "Wants" but not their "needs". They are ready to buy things just to compete "With Joneses" and walk the walk and talk the talk of the rich people and pay homage to their dream of their inner child, they are ready to fly the Aladdin's carpet and lord of know and unknown and shower themselves and loved ones with gifts and extravagant livings of the rich. By their newly received credit cards, they can be happy and careless …

Now you can see, how the demands side of economy include, the "Wasted." The wasted item used only once and shown away, wasted luxuries, and pretended kingdoms and riches.

All of this will push the supply side of the equation to rise and grow, to bulge.

Then everybody working hard to get credit and spend money for items of waste. Factories are busy rolling new lines of cars, vacationers are every where sailing in request for all those new kings and queens.

The economy is good when supply side is high. It brings unemployment down and people are working harder and harder to pay for their credit cards, and finally, for their new cars, houses, stylish cloths, cash is the king.

III. Taxes: In many countries, either there is no direct taxation due to lack of any system or because of having lots of natural resources, people are not really taxed. Government gets their expenses covered with the sale of the country's rich and natural resources. therefore, they do not even bother to collect any taxes from people, or the country is so poor that government tax the people to the brink of nonexistent for their own existence. Therefore, taxes are a phenomenon which can be applied both to harm and to help the people of any county.

These countries who do not tax their countrymen, in reality, they give their people more by not having the proper taxes and this reduces in the demand and waste equation, ultimately reduces the supply. people become a ship without a captain. There is no reason for people to work hard for any tax saving. No need to franchise, no need to incorporation. No need for charity for tax ride offs. On the other hand, there are other countries who double and triple tax their own people. Those people without having a sound law for directing people to work harder but they just make those people to be poorer and less able to buy anything, therefore, lowering the demand factor. But now if taxes are collected with right rules and incentives for the people and corporations such that by doing certain things, they would have to pay less tax. This will be a huge incentive to people use those prescribed laws, such as charities, franchisor, type of workers hired, hours of working.

A "mom & pop" store to avoid his taxes will open another store, therefore, creating jobs for many others. Due to charities paid by big companies many more students will go to college and get education and provide needed services to the society.

With the correct "Tax Rules" you can guide the people in the desired direction, creating jobs by mortgaging existing real state in many countries. There are a lot of real state that long have been paid for and are not producing any wealth for the owners or becoming sole income for millions of people. They are dormant that owner live in them. The owners of those houses have no incentive to work hard for any mortgage, without any mortgage money. Thousand of jobs are lost, and economy suffers tremendously by not putting in circulation the mortgage money.

Just this fact alone could be a huge boost to economy. Some investors or governments would give mortgage loans by charging some interest on the loan which will be attached the loan. The property owners with this money available to invest, thousands of jobs could be created and would help the economy.

The buyers while work hard, both to pay their mortgages and to take care of their investments. Also, with additional taxes which government will be collecting, it could increase the services and new roads and hospitals which in turn will create more work and many thousands of jobs for the people.

1. The Economy of Waste - Concept Elaboration

People for their sustenance need minimum food, clothing, and some sort of transportation. But drinking a very specially brand coffee or exquisite fresh meat or Armenian shish kabob has a high price. We pay for the luxury of the brands not the content (food).

In the same tone to travel from point A to B, any reliable transportation mean will suffice. But when we say we need certain brand of cars, with luxury items or has to be only 1- or 2-years old car, those are additional "wasted" money that we pay for luxury only and it really does not change our goal of going form A to B. Therefore, by creating the artificial demands or so called "Wastes", we create so many jobs and need for employment. Some countries failed to grasp this concept and they force people to drive old beat up cars, no luxury stores or restaurants, no hotels or pleasure houses. By doing this, they reduce their economy since the waste is minimum.

PART I
BUSINESS

2. The Economy of Waste – Powerful Tool of Marketing

With the use of new and powerful theories and with the use of mass media such as: TV, computers, internet, magazines, newspapers, leaflets, coupons, and eventually with the help of slue of professional advertising consultants, people are bombarded with advertising. Those sales gurus have become so professional and goal oriented that they can sell anything to almost anybody in any time of day and night.

People are not secured in any way from those sell agents. They are everywhere, in any system, in house and outside even in shopping centers and malls. They are in living rooms, bathrooms and even in closets. Those advertisement is at work to push an idea, to sell, and worst of all, consumers are fed power bits and comments which your mind sub liminary are automatically being affected by those elements with the slighted inclination. They become so committed to that advertised item, that they eventually decide to buy the item without caring about the value.

Those marketing are so versatile, that like a cat with 9 lives if they cannot sell you an item one way, they surely will discover another way to sell you the same items.

Today marketers are using the latest theories and with advent of computers and "Game Theories" and the universal TV and more media, they are all to portrait anything in a way that are without having that item your life would not have any meaning. He or she will not survive to be the man, be perfect or simply worth it.

The slogan put up with big advertising companies are so that it affects the listener instantly.

A woman listening the sentence "She is worth it" it does not matter what it is or what category it belongs. It is the must have that because, "she is worth it" or not. Today, those catchy phrases are the lighting bulbs for people to buy things from 2-years old kids to old grand dads & moms. Those marketers are so clever and sinister that by inventing those catchy phrases, it is only a matter of time they up surge the sell of any items to astonishing limits of millions and billion dollars sell.

Everything that people can be watching in any place are turned into a billboard for advertising from idle park benches to specific billboards installed in all corners if streets, and highlighted by TV advertising, movies, magazines, coupon books and etc.

For even lightheaded teenagers, the M TV phenomenon has become other form of powerful advertises for all sorts of things. Even, cartoon for kids are not immune from advertising.

Therefore, everything sacred in our life, our heroes and celebrates has been transferred to a walking Bill Boards for advertising for any and or items.

In such a huge rush and power push to sell and make

profits, it does not matter what are you selling, as long as a sell has been done and money is made, and taxes are filled the treasury houses of government. With all this bombardment of advertising with any methods, the manners have become the junk buyer of any sort to satisfy not only their human needs, but also the specific "Wants" of the buyers and sellers. By this, they create an awesome pile of "Waste" items used only once or not used at all, bought in a whim from those multitude of advertised sources. In many cases the "waste" factor of the overall supply equation turning to be much bigger than the "demand' portion.

Supply = Demand + Credit + Waste

This waste potion of the equation makes the economy of the country to be evolved and be robust by creating multitudes of jobs for many and fill the treasury with huge tax funds.

shops are built, skyscrapers are risen to the sky, factories are built in huge warehouses, all of this in one hand helps people by having good paying jobs, cars and all kinds of earthly goodies, but on the other hand creates lots of waste in the nation. Creating filthy smoggy air, full of waste toxic lands and rivers, reducing the ozone layers, climate warming, forests are cut down, and above all, the morality of people and nations have declined due to tremendous pressure to acquire much more money.

The people have become very sophisticated robots with extremely focused in their goals of making more of the all the mighty dollars so, that they can buy more and more of wasted items for sell. Because of this phenomenon and lack of "time" or better said lack of more time to make money vs. spending time for their family relationships and personal and social growth, everything become fast food and TV and newspaper buying advertisement. Kids become teenagers in much younger ages and teenagers become men and women with real responsibility in incredibly young age.

16-year-olds first get their driver license, then get employed then become employer in a job. So, they can pay for their car expenses and many other express like buying of all these wasted items had been sold to them. Therefore, it transforms an innovative kid to a responsible teenage adult with all the worries and responsibilities of the adults. Losing their innocent childhood and teenaged years, no more childhood games and endless times for play and bonding, no more storytelling by grandmas, no more time to learn right and wrongs, no more family gathering with grandmas and grandpas, no more endless time for fishing and camping. Everything is reduced to capsules of exceedingly small times for the social activities, rest is used to acquire and consume all mighty dollars.

The society 'shame" and "Honor' disappears giving its way to a cold and heartless requirements and laws in the books. The lawyers and judges interpreted the laws without time for consideration. People change to numbers and accounts. With powerful computers and use of those numbers and accounts, at any moments big and small companies including the government, know exact status of any one of those peoples their accounts and ownerships. Arm with this invaluable information, they know all about you; your buying habits, your spending habit, your status in society, type of item you will be interested in, type of food and facial cream you use and so on. They use this information to sell you all the items that you need and want or dream about with their marketing techniques. So, you buy and buy and spend and spend till the day you die. Most of these items, you have bought is either wasted in garbage bags or corner of house and garages. Most homeowners turn their garages to a big storage house for items bought and not used really, waiting for the day a need will come for their use. This special day almost never arrives or it ever if it did, you have long forgotten about the purchased items. You are more apt to buy that needed item from store where you know you can find, rather to look in the piles of junk items in garage for that specific item.

3. The Economy of Waste: Advertising

There are huge economic gains and jobs in field of advertising today, but this has a huge, wasted time and money associated with it for people. Today the advertisers by use of new technology although they are making huge sums of money, but they create havoc in people's life by taking away their time and peace of mind. Those advertising companies by use of emails, Texts, Calls, Social Media, Websites, TV and Radio are constantly bombarding people's cellphones, emails, and their social media such as Facebook, tweeters, Instagram etc. with their advertisements and goods or services for sale. Meanwhile, some savvy computer or cellphone hackers create other kinds of nuisance and money grabbing skims to take away people's money, time, and peace of mind. Those advertises by using freedom of speech laws are abusing people instead making their pockets full. All these wasted time, money and peace of mind can be prohibited by having strict laws for the advertisers to do their advertising in certain way and in specified time. People have this erroneous idea that freedom of speech is limitless, but they are not aware that any freedom becomes heart ache when it in fringes in someone else's freedom. Due to the huge money made by big advertising companies and the companies behind those advertising agencies, do everything that nobody can limit their advertisement all day long. Therefore, this wasted economy should be somehow organized in better way to help people gain their piece of mind and their freedom, at the same time get important information they need to have.

4.   The Economy of the Waste: Bottled Water & Beverages

The economy of waste is encircled in all aspects of life, therefore, even something so simple as drinking water has been used by clever businessmen to create a huge economy out of nowhere. They have taken a good water from the faucets which is available in any household, restaurant and public places by use of clever advertising by taking the same water and even making it worse by taking all the minerals out of the system and they sell you "purified" water as if it is good for you. Additionally, they profit majorly this way by charging you more than what it is supposed to cost. Also, some of their advertising include mixing of the water with other additives, some good, some bad and some claim it is organic components, vitamins, however others contain artificial dyes and flavors. By use of beautifully designed bottles in and shape and form, large or small, they sell those same waters that you would have for free, for huge profits. Although, this bottling system creates jobs and some sort of an economy, however, it is an economy of waste because it's not a newly created economy, but they use the same water that our forefathers have been drinking for centuries, except these entrepreneurs are now making money from it. The sad truth about their methods entails reverse osmosis, which takes the water and faucet water and wastes few gallons to give you one gallon of purified water. This is tremendous because the households that buy the systems of this reverse osmosis are going to get more purified water without understanding that amount of wasted water which goes in the sewer and they pay for that also and the end result is they are getting one gallon of purified water that has no minerals, which are useful for our bodies. The tragedy is, areas like California, which is in a constant drought, imagine the millions of households, wasting few gallons of water to get one gallon of purified water. This is tremendous waste and it's a tragedy that our governmental agencies are ignoring this major loses and instead they are forcing households to cut on water the trees and greenery, encouraging people to remove their trees and greenery and install artificial lawns and gardens and rock field yards, which creates a havoc on the atmosphere, on production of oxygen and it worsens the drought situation by not having enough moisture in the air. Therefore, although in one way those entrepreneurs created a business for themselves by bottling those waters and selling it for profit in other ways, they are damaging the whole ecosystem and helping the drought more. The other aspect of the economy of waste is wasted and trashed plastic bottles all over the place and all our landfills are filled with those bottles, which they do not degrade, and it takes centuries to deteriorate. Our oceans are filled with those plastic bottles and they are killing and hurting marine life and creating a huge problem for the authorities on how to clean up these oceans and landfills and this in itself will need billions of dollars (wasted dollars) to do the cleanup but remember out of these wasted dollars we are going to create a job for a few.

The same story goes about all bottled beverages. Although, over the surface, the businessmen who came up with these drinks to enhance peoples drinking habits and entice their taste buds and make life interesting but in reality, they created a huge economy with a huge tab for the health hazard. In the last thirty years, type II diabetes have increased in numbers because children and adults are consuming tremendous amounts of these tasteful drinks which are nothing but water and lots of sugar up to 40% at times and other additives, such as caffeine, high fructose corn syrup, sodium cyclamate, and BPA. These are all harmful and heavily addicting for the body. Those beverages, like the bottled waters are consumed by people who pay lots of money by contaminating their bodies with these excessive sugars and above-mentioned additives. Also, the plastic bottles create the same havoc on the environment as the bottled waters do. The other cost is the health care issue, which by consuming these heavily sugary drinks the concern for type II diabetes is at large and is something that is happening when people are carelessly consuming these products. The health costs itself, which is tremendous in billions of dollars, we did not have this issue even thirty years ago and because of this wasted economy, now pharmaceutical companies, which they do cures for those man-made eels, they come up with pills that one should take every day to help one's diabetic situation and imagine how much money these companies are profiting by targeting these individuals. These are only a few multimillion profits out of our sickness, which was created with clever businessmen for their own profits. The sad truth is that our government has washed up their hands to regulate those companies that they should not sell beverages say more than 5% sugar but those companies are so huge and profitable that by their huge donations to government agencies and elections, they have the last say on how they are going to produce their material, after all it is a free country and everybody himself or herself decides what they want to drink and in what levels, although they never think of all the consequences they are creating for themselves and their families and all the money they are paying for health insurance. This is a vivid indication of the economy of waste which is created by few greedy and careless individual just for profits and using our laws to enhance their pockets.

Energy drinks are another aspect of those drinks that have so much of other additives such as caffeine, Guarana, which is known as Brazilian coca, sugars, taurine, ginseng and B vitamins and other additives. Those drinks have become so popular with specially youth that they abuse it a lot and this way they create hypertension, diabetics type II, and usually people who use those drinks get addicted to them due to its caffeine contents so much that they cannot operate normally before consuming those drinks. Besides health issues, they spend a lot of money to buy those drinks which is another aspect of Waste of Economy. Sadly, are few government rules or other agencies such as CDC to control over usage of those drinks. Business companies advertise those dangerous drinks with having only goal of selling to make more profit regardless of the harm they are causing to people. On the other hand, the officials are not calling those drinks as drugs, therefore, they are unable to control their production and sells no matter how much hurt and heartache it creates for people and tremendous amount of money are spent on hospitals and health system.

5.   The Economy of Waste: Cheap Goods from China

In the last decade, China with its cheap labor has been producing cheap priced goods of any sorts such as clothing, furnishing, cars, tools, equipment, machinery etc. with a such low prices that all the countries in the world have been rushing there to get their goods or ordering them online. Although, the goods from China are cheap in price but the quality is also exceptionally lower. This phenomenon, of buying cheap and lower quality goods from China with such a huge market has created a total economy of waste matter. People in every country love to buy those cheap once in a time use items because everybody can afford to buy those items regardless of their quality. People have learned that buying cheap is good and affordable, but they forget about the cost of buying the same items many more time because it easily breaks down and gets wasted so one has to buy another one to replace it. There is this wise English saying, "I am not rich enough to buy cheap things," which is so true that when you buy cheap goods, with less quality, it breaks down easily and get wasted quickly so you have to replace the same item few more times. Therefore, it is mostly advisable to buy things with quality and value, so you do not need to replace the same items constantly. This way although you pay more upfront, but it pays at the end which is you spend less money for a longer period of use. China cheap goods phenomena, has such a huge effect on the economies of the world that many countries including United States, have stopped building or producing millions of goods in the country because it is much cheaper to buy the same items produced in China with even paying the shipping fees. The huge problem is that since countries do not produce the machinery and goods in the country, it creates lots of unemployment both in labor and highly educated sectors. People in the country becoming the users or sellers in business and they are no manufacturing or creation of goods in those countries. The other scary scenario is that if one day China decides to stop producing or selling certain goods, lots of countries and people will be in hardship for that item and the price of the item will be immediately increased many folds or due to lack of that item in time of emergencies, will create panic and death in those societies. As we experienced in the time of pandemic with lack of basic but at the same time necessary items such as masks, alcohol, hand sanitizers and toilet paper, ventilators etc. Could you imagine that one day America will be running out of those basic items that people panic so much and they had to herd in stores and markets to acquire those basic items and sometimes pay three- or four-times higher price for the same simple item. Hence, we should learn from this pandemic experience. Firstly, buying all your goods from outside countries is a bad idea for business of that country. Secondly, the use of those cheap items cost more for people in the long term. Therefore, countries and people should be wise enough to buy things in its value, not only for its cheap price but also its value for the economy of the country through thick and thin.

6.   The Economy of Waste: Re-design

Re-designing, has become the new norms of selling and advertising of items, creating buyers just because they need to have the latest version of that certain item although that revision may or may not have any added value or enhancement of the item. The businessmen and companies with big budgets for advertising sell the same items with minor changes to the buying and hungry customers for the new version of the item with a big price tag. This creates another version of economy of waste where money is wasted on the same item, the same quality and value, with a higher price. Clever companies and advertising agencies sale the same items with higher price this time by changing the color, retooling portion of the item or changing the size and shape and design. Items such as cosmetics with their new colors, shines, new bottle shapes and sizes, are sold to hungry customers who wants the latest cosmetics buy, charging their credit cards for those revised and renamed items. The same cars with the same engine and body are reworked on by changing their lights, interior, the color shades, addition of minimum safety items or new hubcaps are sold with much higher prices. This re-design phenomenon is such a prevalent in every aspect of society that is one of the major ways of selling the same item to customers with a much higher price. The wasted economy in this is that people charge their high interest credit cards just to buy the same items which they do not get any additional value of it but they pay higher price and got into debt more.

7. The Economy of Waste: Construction

Although, there is lots of waste in construction, one aspect of it is that wasted energy through the walls and money spent on heating and air conditioning of the buildings. The wasted economy on this particular case is buildings build with insufficient insulations, cause the heating and air condition units to work much harder and longer hours to cool or heat the residence, therefore, wasting lots of energy and money paid for utilities and upgrading and repairing of those unites. Although, this repair work and utility payments create some work and employment, but essentially it is more waste than the economy it provides. The design of residence with high-tech industry and engineering should be such that energy is not wasted for the buildings. This could be accomplished by providing better insulation in walls and floors of the wood constructed building, or rather than wood try to use other means of construction such as concrete structures to reduce need for insulations. This simple solution will reduce the amount of energy used by heating and air conditioning units and saving millions of dollars country wide. Historically, residential buildings are built by 2x4 studs which is 1.5x3.5-inch studs' size, which incorporates an insulation of rating R13 or R15. By increasing the stud size to 2x6 one can use R19 or R30 insulations which is much better insulation and will help to save energy and wasted money. I am sure, there is better methods and designs for this purpose but because contractors are used to the old system, it is extremely hard to change to this new method of construction. The other aspect of this wasted economy is all the old buildings and residences without proper insulation. The government agencies should come up with a practical and less costly methods to insulate those old buildings which will be both helpful to create jobs and employment on this new venture and spend money to buy and install those new insulations, this would be a onetime pay but will save the customers thousands in coming years by reducing the utility payment and repairs on heat and air condition unites.

8.   The Economy of Waste: Ethics in business

In a capitalistic system were business means profit, and there is no business without profit, some businessmen have forgotten the ethics in business and all they remember is how to expand their profit. The companies to enlarge their profits, they use and abuse people and other companies whom they get services from. Although, those businesses waste millions of dollars on luxury and take huge sums out of the business for their own use by having luxury boats, cars, and houses etc. and all under written for expenses of the company. Those businessmen forget about equality and ethics in business and they are trying to get as much as they can from others and from their own employees rather than being fair and ethical to others. Although, business is for profit, but the profit has a limit and one should not overstep the limits, causing harm and degradation of people who work for them. Those illegal use of company money for their own use and their lavish lifestyles many help the economy by spending on those expensive goods meanwhile, it pushes their employees to work harder, to get second job in order to survive. Those businessmen who spend millions for advertising their business and try to bribe the authorities and other service men to enhance their business, they forget that one of the best advertising of their business would be having happy employees who work hard and happily on their jobs and those clients who feel like not taken advantage of being lied to. Those customers knowing that businessmen they work with have ethics therefore, they feel much connected to the business and can easily recommend other people to use the service of that business. In this type of relationship, the businessman does not need to spend thousands of dollars on advertising because word of mouth is enough to bring lots of customers. As an example, we can look at the extraordinarily successful business of some well-known hamburger places, although they are very successful business in sales of high quality hamburgers and French fries, with satisfied customers lining up in cars for a block to order their food, but there are many wastes that needs to be pointed out. First, all those customers in cars lining for a block to get their food, waste their time and energy, the gasoline in the car, waiting many minutes for their order. Second, bunch of young employees are jammed in a small kitchen, cooking and preparing food for customers in a very hectic and under pressure condition which economically make sense and the pay is dissent but we're putting our youth in such a stressful situation that can easily be remedy by enlarging the kitchen or having second kitchen in a row. In the first scenario by providing enough parking people do not have to wait in their cars while the engine is running wasting lots of gasoline. In futuristic setting, if the parking is limited then it can be enlarged by use of new elevated parking system.

PART II

FAMILIES

9. The Economy of Waste: Families

In the United States of America, the families could be said they are a great example of "The Economy of Waste." In a typical family, husband and wife work, little kids are sent to daycares or babysitters are taking care of them, elder kids are in school that usually school provides their meals, and they have after school programs to take care of them up to 6:00pm, when the family is back from work and can pick them up and take them home. Teenagers, after age 16 get their driving license and with their parent's help, they buy a car so they can be independent to get to school and to work. Usually, those teenagers work part time during the week, or they work weekends. Let us look the whole picture; because mom works, then they need a babysitter, a daycare or school to take care of them. This phenomenon cost a lot and the expenses are paid by family and taxpayers for extended school hours. The wage that mother brings is really spent on taking care of kids while she is out to work. Also, since mom is working then she needs to pay much more for own dresses and upkeep and having an extra car with all its expenses of gas money, insurance, car payment and car maintenance. If you look closely all that hoopla about mother working economically does not make sense, since her income is all spent on items that she would not have spent if she stayed home and take care of the kids. On the other hand, when mother work, kids loose enough attention and care during the day which cause them separation and alienation between members of a family. Therefore, all that effort that moms put to go to work is wasted energy and money to gain wages which are wasted to cover expenses anyway, and kids are shorthanded for their mom love and care. Teenagers, because mom is at work and they need to attend to school and work, become drivers of their own cars with all responsibilities and cost, which most of the time their income is not enough to cover those expense therefore, family pitches in. those teenagers lose their precious time of studying and having a careless life instead, they go to work for having income. Other sad aspect of this phenomena is, because of their youth and inexperience they get involved in many accidents which sometimes cause them their life or serious lifetime injures and lots of hospital bills. Looking from above, we see that how much of waste is in as far as teens becoming drivers because of mom working. The growth of the economy is related to this phenomenon of mom working, kids taking cared by others and teens driving. The economy grows because the family needs two extra cars for mom and teenager therefore, they get loan, pay taxes, insurances, maintenance, gas, etc. this way, lots of people are employed to provide those services. Therefore, the economy of the country is partially dependent on this above-mentioned phenomenon. In other less developed countries mom does not work, teenager do not drive, kids are not being watched by babysitters every day because, mom or a family member which live with them in the same household, is taking care of the kids. By doing this the economy of those countries shrink and unemployment is extremely high. The mere fact that less cars are driven and there are no manufacturing to produce those cars and there are less accidents and less traffic and ultimately they do not build so many freeways, highways, bridges, wider roads, traffic polices and annual repairs necessary for upkeep of those roads. That is the reason that economy is shrink and there are less employment and workplace.

10. The Economy of Waste – Luxury VS. Waste

In today's society, luxury items have become the ultimate goal of people, It is not the "Need" that drives people to buy the necessary items but to the "Wants" of people to have the best and the luxurious cars, clothing, etc. This apathy to acquire luxurious items with the natural tendencies of human beings to have a rivalry among them and try to excel and walk with the" Joneses" makes them to buy the items with credit cards for sure. It does not matter they can afford or not. No more it is the matter of survival, but it is all the "Wants" of life and Self-gratification and the ego driven society, that makes them to buy and buy and even not think any consequences. There is no shame of bankruptcy and shame of being pointed for having the worst credit scores or the expose of town's people with this need attitude, they use their credit to buy more things even by Jeopardizing their future. They even mortgage their homes to pay for those luxury items. As it is obvious these buying frenzy excels the country's economy.

11. The Economy of Waste – The Happiness Factor

Although people work long hours; hard work and jobs with full of stress, still they are happy that they can earn the mighty dollars. This phenomenon is so strange and ridiculous that one thinks why the same person being mostly immigrants in the US, in their own country they would not work even half as hard on most of the jobs that they gladly do in USA, they would not even contemplate to do it at all. It seems that in their own society the factor of shame the factor of belonging and notion of the government should provide for them is so high, that it prevents them from working hard.

"Las Vegas" a waste economy in this never sleeping gambling town has become a mecca for all kinds of other forms of entertainment to lure the public to their town. One of the vivid kinds of these entertainments which is also a great source of economy of waste is the construction of exotic building in the shapes and sizes of famous world structures and monuments. This creates a huge demand from public to see those luxurious structures with a huge economy of tourists traveling to this unique city and spending millions of dollars. Another form of their economy is that just for the sake of attracting the gamblers and self-seekers almost a new building is torn down in order to build a new structure in its place just to please more and more customers. One would think why not leave the original structure alone in its place, which is useful and almost new and could be used for many useful and government charity building or public housing and instead building that new casino in other location. But no, is that certain location of mentioned casino so important that rather waste and spend million more to remove the old structure and build new one in the same city location. The building is not old or useless, but it is a hinderance to attract more customers. This then become example of our "Economy of Waste" and by constructing a new building, we help the economy circle and create more demand.

12. The Economy of Waste: Car Lease

Today, due to people being so busy with work that in each family having only one car is not working. Therefore, family members are also required to have a car to be able to drive to work, school, gym etc. It is extremely hard for any given family to own multiple cars with high payments, so, rather than buying that car they would lease it from the car dealerships. Now the "Economy of Waste" comes because rather than owning the car and paying it off in few years and own it clear, dealers have come up with a clever way of leasing their cars to people. The lease includes lots of interest payment and a residual amount at the end of the lease. As a result, people instead of buying a car, they lease the same car with a smaller payment since they are not paying to own the car but to own only portion of the car for certain period of the time. The lease amount paid for few years is all lost when the lease is over. At the end of the lease, one has the option to buy the same leased car for the residual amount and other additional fees for repairs and upgrades of the car. In one-way people are happy to lease because they are getting a brand-new car with much smaller monthly payments but on the other hands most of the payment amount are lost when the lease is over. So, they must pay again to buy the car. Also, when the lease is over one must pay for repairs and upkeeps and for additional charges for extra mileages over the limit specified in the lease. This way, car dealers sell millions of cars and they make lots of profits and buyers are also happy to drive brand new cars for limited time without noticing the wasted money in or economy of waste.

13. The Economy of Waste: Multiple Cars in Families

Another facet of economy of waste is that families are made to acquire multi cars due to lack of enough public transportation due to greed of oil companies, (seven sisters) and the government inaptitude to provide efficient public transportation for all of the people. Also, a huge advertising is behind the scenes to encourage people to drive their own car with lots of pride and enjoyment rather than taking the bus or other public transportation if there are any. Having multiple cars in the family creates a havoc on family's finances and city transportation and environment. Those issues such as care lease payment, insurance payment, repairs, accidents, traffic tickets, washing and cleaning the care and finally the use of gas for driving the car, creates an immense need for capital. Therefore, all the family members to be able to use their cars they must work hard and spend lots of their family time working for somebody else with many different working shifts. One can see that due to this phenomenon people are working hard for the privilege of driving their own cars rather than using transportation. The wasted economy, shines when people by using good public transportation they do not need to slave themselves to their cars, instead spend quality time with their families and friends, and do not get aggravated because of lack of money or jobs to pay for their car expenses.

14. The Economy of Waste: House Remodeling

The Economy of waste is nicely elaborated with phenomenon of remodeling the house and walking and talking as do the "Joneses." Families specially new immigrants, young and old, as soon as they buy a house no matter what condition the house is it's their obligation and life mission to change, remodel, paint, redecorate, alter rooms and bathrooms, remodel or rebuild a new kitchen and bathrooms, reroof existing not so old roof, create new landscape, remove existing concrete or paving to match their "wants," their dreams and all the efforts to match the "Joneses" or their friends and relatives. Most of the time, there is no "Need" to do all the above-mentioned remodeling and spending lots of money to do this work. This is a part of "Economy of the Waste" when they really do not need to do all these remodeling and spend thousands of dollars but other hand the "Want" kick in along with the mighty advertising hands of sellers, dealers, construction companies and repair service men to do the remodeling of their house. This remodeling needed or wanted creates a huge economy and working for the people. Although, this remodeling expenditure is good for economy and creation of jobs but, it forces the homeowners and their families to work much harder to be able to afford the payments of this remodeling which is usually done by high interest credit cards or by taking a loan against the house which usually jeopardizes the ownership of the house.

In many countries, the economy is dead because the owners of the houses rarely do the wanted remodeling, they are satisfied doing only minimum required repairs. Therefore, there is no incentive for homeowners and their family members to work hard to be able to pay for un-necessary remodeling and by doing this they deprive all the construction companies, dealerships, hardware and supply stores, handymen and other service people to work and earn money. That is the reason the economy of those countries is down and there are few progresses made, also, there are lots of unemployment and poor people around. It is an irony that in time of this global pandemic of COVID-19 at which most people stayed home being unemployed, somehow the "Wants" in people kicked in and they spend lots of money and labor to do lots of needed and un-necessary remodeling of their homes which this phenomenon created many jobs and sell of hardware helping the economy at this special time. Sometimes, governments in order to boost the economy, and feed the "Wants" of people, they give money directly to people so, they can spend on whatever they want to boost the economy by buying and spending this government gift.

15. The Economy of Waste: Branding

The phenomena of "Branding" have been hipped so much that every company now tries to get brand's name for its goods. People have been learned and instructed that without brands their values and their standing in society will diminish so much that they must have that brand name on their position. Therefore, they pay tremendous amount of money to acquire the goods with brand's name on it. A Woman waking in the mall or streets if she is not wearing that certain brands of clothing, jewelry, shoes, and bags, she feels less important and frown upon or simply miserable in the eyes of onlookers. This phenomenon is not only for clothing but is also for jewelries, watches, shoes, bags, cars etc. the hype in having the brand name is so much that people get into huge debts to get that certain brand-named items. One pays triple or more to acquire the same basic car with certain name associated with it. By doing this they are getting into debt by leasing or buying that car by monthly payment of more than their ability to pay. Therefore, they have sacrificed their peace time hours to work more or cut hour from their family time and expectation grows that all the family members should work just to pay those heavy payments. The effect of this type of thinking is pushing people to work harder just to be able to pay for the brand items of their desire. Although those companies having brand names in their possession make millions of dollars in sales, they are forcing people to work hard, to get into huge debts just to pay their payments. It is sad to see that the same shoes without a brand name is as good as the brand name version of it but due to its hyped people duped to buy the brand name one, without consideration of its quality or value they are getting for it. The wasted economy in this matter is so huge that the winner is the brand name carrier and the financial institutions with their visa and master card with high interest of 20% or more. This way they make slaves out of the ordinary people and overburden them with lots of unnecessary debts.

16. The Economy of Waste: Wasted Trash

Another notion of wasted economy is the buying of the cheap and less valued items from China, give people the feeling that since those items are cheap, they can be wasted, abused, and throw away because it is easy to replace them. This concept of throwing away and wasting items creates another dilemma for the country and its environment which is accumulation of lots of waste that needs to be shipped from homes to landfills. This process creates lots of waste of energy, gasoline, and labor for picking up those items and filling in the trucks, transporting them to landfills and fill those landfills with those wasted items which creates another havoc on the environment. The plastic used in protecting those cheap items and subsequently removing and trashing them out, has such a huge adverse effect on environment because the plastic does not disintegrate and will stay for a long time in landfills or as it's common in the oceans causing damages and killing fishes and other species.

17. The Economy of Waste: Credit Cards

Credit cards are the best enforcer and creator of economic activity in most of developed countries. It alone improves the economy of the country by extremely high margins. What is credit card? A plastic that gives you the power to spend to your heart's desire. The more credit card a person has, the more options he/she must spend for items of needs or wants. The beauty of this plastic card is that one does not have to pay the full amount every month instead one pays only small portion of the amount spent as "Minimum Payment." That gives the person having that credit card spend on items that usually he would not be able to spend. Also, imagine the power one feels when he/she can buy items that usually rich people buy, and he/she always wished for. That is the reason, in develop countries it is harder to distinguish spending habits of rich and poor. Sometimes, low-income people wear highly desired brands of clothing and shoes and drive the latest model of expensive cars that high income people may not have them. People high- or low-income earners, go to the same restaurant, bars, and casinos as if they are all rich and there is no difference between them. The young people specially they do not care when they are going to pay off those high interest rate credit cards because their monthly payments are adjusted by their lifestyle and income. Those clever credit card companies which charge very high interest rates on those credit cards, they do not care that you pay the credit balance soon and they actually love to extend life of your credit with your minimum payment because the longer you have the credit balance the more, they earn on their money. The interest rates commonly charge for these cards are more than 20 percent, which is a huge income for the credit card companies. The economy of those developed countries expands immensely due to their fellow citizens ability to spend and acquire goods and luxury items per their needs or wants. The value of sells is so high that both companies and their employees are satisfied with their income and therefore, being able to spend more themselves so the economy grows and grows. In undeveloped countries, credit cards are rare, and people are not aware of the use, advantage, and disadvantages of those plastic cards "Credit Cards." Because of this people use cash only to do their errands and even buying a costly big item are done through cash or through their checking accounts. Therefore, if one does not have cash money would not be able to buy items in needs so the person must wait months and years to save some money to be able to buy the same item which now the price has gone up. Also, due to unavailability of credit card, people spend much less, they do not go to luxury restaurants or entertainment centers or basic shopping for not only their needs but also for their desires. Because of handicap in spending the economy of those countries shrinks and instead of robust economy they end up with poor economy with lots of unemployment, old cars in streets, houses in bad shapes and extended family members all live in a small house together so they can save some money for their future. By introducing this concept of credit cards, those countries slowly will expand their economy and reduce their unemployment because of additional sells of goods and services due to credit being available for people to use for their needed and wanted goods.

In Fact, the "Waste of Economy" in above scenario can be obviously seen in both situations in highly developed and undeveloped countries. In developed countries the wasted economy comes about because of people work harder and spend most of their time on acquiring salaries to pay for those unwanted luxury items and fruitless expenditure for unnecessary items, goods, gifts, gambling, expensive restaurants, and vacations. Those people do not have enough time for themselves or their families to spend together and enjoy their family time. Since, staring from the youth, they work, they miss their childhood years and become slaves to lifelong of hard work and miss the real aspect of their life which is having time with family, going to sporting events, movie theaters, shows, opera, waking in museums with their kids and so on. On the other hand, in undeveloped countries the "Economy of Waste" is apparent, when one sees how people live in a miserable condition in a ruined houses, dirt and narrow roads, old cars, lack of beautiful restaurants or entertainment center, lack shopping centers, luxury goods, not being able to entertain their imagination and wants, not being able to go to buy things that they desire. People spend their youth and most of their lifetime just dreaming for their heart-desires and since they cannot get it, they feel unsatisfied and always jealous of people in other countries that have those luxuries. They can see those luxuries in movies, TV shows, internet and magazines which makes them feel inferior human beings and they accumulate some hate rate or jealousy towards those countries, or they blame their own country's governments for not doing enough to expand the economy so their earnings and employment could increase. This phenomenon is the reason that one can see lots of immigrations from undeveloped countries to develop countries. People want to acquire all those goods that they see in media through internet and since they do not have it in their countries and they are not able to get it, therefore, they go through the hardship and the hell of traveling in miserable conditions through deserts, sea or woods to reach their dreamland, and when they get there they spend years to learn the new ways of living and trying to be part of the new society, always remembering their homeland and connections and all the missed love of their friends and family members. Those first-generation immigrants never-recovered emotionally and always are in between the two cultures.

18. The Economy of Waste: Loans

Loans are a great means of helping people to acquire housing and businesses. People go to their bank and ask for a loan to buy a house. Banks first check their credits of the home buyers and based on their credit, they increase or decrease the interest rate for the loan. Also, banks ask for initial down payments for buying the house and these down payments are usually between 3 to 20 percent of the buying price, after which banks check the income of the perspective buyers to see if they can make the payments of the house loan usually, the payment should be about 25 to 30 percent of monthly gross income. Those loans are given for periods of 10, 15, 20, 25 or 30 years with specific interest rates. A perspective homeowner, rather than rent an apartment or a house for few year which all the rent payments are lost and is still homeless then thinks about how to be able to buy a home so all the payments he/she makes goes toward reducing the loan amount and eventually after that specific time he becomes the paid in full home owner. Lots of people do not have the full amount necessary to buy a house out right. Therefore, they only provide the required down payment amount and the rest they get a long-term loan through the bank. This way the buyer is happy that he/she has a home and knows that after few years the house will be fully paid, he/she will be the sole owner and can transfer the house to the family member after he/she is passing or can sell the house before end of the term. Usually, since sometime is passed from the day they bought the house equity increases and the owner gain profit from selling the house so he/she can buy a new bigger house with the sell proceeds. By having this type of loan with a interest rates much lower than credit cards in the range of 5 percent, people are able to buy a house and after few years gain equity and use that equity to buy new houses, use the equity to buy business or use it for their children's college or university tuition. The "Waste of Economy" in this situation is the cases where the economy fluctuates and there is inflation and the variable interest rates in some loans changes and becomes much higher, therefore making the house payments much larger. In some cases, some homeowners cannot make their payments with the high interest rates so they either sell the house with much less price or lose the house to the bank who owns the loan. Either way he/she loses all the equity and the monthly payment made for the house. Those people end up wasting all their time and money paid for their house which is the" Waste of Economy" in this situation.

Businessmen, by getting loans from banks they buy businesses, build building or warehouses for their businesses or they get the loan to improve and expand their business. With doing this small business can acquire land, buildings, equipment for their businesses, pay for advertising or relocation, etc., these loans therefore, are ladder for improvement and expansion of the businesses. When a business is expanded it requires more employees and they can produce more products and this way they can help the economy of the country. The "Waste of Economy" for businesses is that by getting the loan, to start or expand their businesses, if those loans have high interest rates or they are variable or it is due in a shorter period, the business is in jeopardy and owners are in the risk of losing the business. When this happens, the business owners lose their equity in the business, all the equipment and furniture either lose or sell in cheaper price. Some businessmen never recover the loss, and they need their businesses or their livelihood, others may file for bankruptcy to get rid of their accumulated debts. The bankruptcy has lots of negative aspects including the trauma the businessmen and their family go through it and They cannot recover their credit for seven years so they will not be able to get any new loans to start over. Also, when someone files for bankruptcy the credit holders' banks or individuals lose lots of money because of it. This phenomenon becomes a waste of economy and shrinks the progress of the economy.

PART III

HEALTCARE

19. The Economy of Waste: Healthcare

As we all know, the amount of money we spend on our healthcare is the highest in the world. With such tremendous amount of spending, I do not think we are getting the best of care and services from our insurance companies, health providers, government, or other agencies. All these points out to huge amount of waste which is hidden in the system.

At this point, we are not advocating government system of providing health but the current system of using insurance companies to provide healthcare for us. The amount of waste is everywhere in every aspect of healthcare and services. First of all, if you have a small sickness, you first need to contact the insurance provider to see if you are eligible then you need to see your primary doctor which will take a few weeks to get an appointment then after appointment she/he cannot perform or do the basic checkup because he needs to get the authorization from insurance companies or providers to be able to do those basic checkups. After that, patients get approval letters in few weeks to go to certain hospitals or labs to do the basic checkup tests asked by the primary doctor and wait another few days for doctors to receive the result then make another appointment for you to go see the primary doctor to discuss the findings from the test. Now let us examine the waste and the time wasted for all those appointments and preliminary tests. In most countries, when you see your primary doctor, most of preliminary tests such as urine and blood check is done in house and the results are ready for doctor to review and write you a diagnoses and proscription to get. This system is so wasteful that people spend lots of time and money and getting off the work for this stupid appointment. Therefore, simplifying the procedure will eliminate lots of waste. The other huge waste in this system is that since the doctor does not have enough time to check the patient because of so much required paperwork, they prescribe either minimum amount of medication or medication which are less effective so it would not create problems for patient at the same time with the low dosage of the medicine, pharmacist will sell much more of the same medicine for a prolong cure time. That is the reason, people are used to having this low dosage medicine along with many more vitamins to help their health situation for many years. All these wasted medicine, vitamins and unnecessary procedures could be eliminated if doctors had enough time to examine the patient and diagnose proper medicine and cure for the patient without being the agent the pharmacist to diagnose those low dosage pills and vitamins. Unfortunately, the money wasted in this health system is so huge that pharmaceutical companies spend billions of dollars to advertise any kind of medicine, being natural, organic or over the counter medicines and vitamins. This industry with its huge dollar amount and advertising immense budget spent billions to feed people unnecessary pills and ointments and so on. The waste in this huge market is such that people spend millions of dollars on items un-necessary for their health or their longevity. The people unknowingly when they listen or see the advertisement for such organic pills or ointment which will supposedly enhance their looks and their health, or they hear from a friend who used the same medicine, and she/he had such a wonderful result that right away she/he goes to order the same item. In all these cases there is no government agency or other higher-level agencies that could organize the system. Therefore, all those sales go under democratic freedoms and it is the right of people to buy whatever they are pleased with. By use of a single system, either implemented by government or and insurance company and by giving doctors more leeway to do their work and have laboratories close by doctor's offices this will eliminate waste of time and money for unnecessary appointments and medications. Let us take another issue which is emergence of diabetic type II in our society which was non heard of since 1960s. The diabetic type II started when companies without regards of people's health, just to sell their foods, they added sugar in every kind of food and drinks. Now a days most of the soft drinks contains 5 to 40 percent sugar. The food in restaurants and pastries are full of sugar regardless of the damage they are causing to people's health. All these are done without government's supervision and control. They use the freedom of speech to do any kind of advertisement to sell those sugar filled items. Therefore, creating a havoc on people's health which doctors, and pharmacists love it since it creates more patient, more medicine sells and higher earning for those involved.

20. The Economy of Waste: Doctors

It is so sad to see that Doctors which their primary care was their patients, and they try hard to healthier sickness by really checking their physical and mental health by examining them closely, by touching and measuring their vital signs and ask lots of question about their eating and sleeping habits and finally based of all those discoveries they would prescribe certain medicine to cure their illness. Again, as the big companies and lawyers have created a havoc in our health industry by introducing so many laws, procedures and amendments that doctors spend more time on paper works, filling up different forms that they have no spare time to spend analyzing patients. Also, because of those many frugal and waste of time lawsuits brought up by those hungry lawyers and greedy people asking for lots of money out of no-where the cost for patients have increased tenfold and the quality of doctors to examine and diagnose proper drugs have diminished so much that the trust of doctors by their patients have disintegrated. The simple act of doctors seeing their patients have become the huge case of paperwork, useless lab procedures, and high-tech ultrasound and MRI usage for the slightest cut or bruises because of possibility of lawsuits. Doctors prescribe lots of tests, procedures and vitamins and useless medicine just to indicate to lawyers and hospitals they have done their outmost to check and control the condition of patients prior to prescribing any medicine.

The economy of waste on this matter is so much that people spend thousands of dollars, either from their own pockets or through their highly paid insurance to deal with this paperwork, lab-work and other non-sense forms filled because of possibility of lawsuits. Although, having that high-tech equipment in laboratories and hospitals have helped lots of patients to recover from their sickness but, the abuse of those systems has created tremendous const for doctors and healthcare systems overall. Not many patients truly need those high-tech interventions for their sicknesses but, because of possibility of lawsuits and slightest shortcomings doctors readily prescribe those high-tech tests and procedures. The wasted economy in this matter is such a huge cost to patients and healthcare facilities but in other hands, it creates some employment and high paid jobs for others. Another aspect of this Economy of Waste, is that patients need to cut their working hours in order to go to visit a doctor, waiting hours in waiting rooms before they see doctors and get their prescriptions to go to do their laboratory work which intern takes another appointment and hours waste to do the procedures, meanwhile, taking minimum use medicines till lab results are given to doctors so they now can prescribe the proper medicine. A common cold could cost patient few days off the work plus insurance payments, and medicine expense. As we can see in this example, a common cold which was just to rest and take over the counter medicine for a few days, nowadays it includes all the above-mentioned lab works and wasted time which make the patient to work harder and long hours to pay for that extra services.

21. The Economy of Waste: Elderly Care

The economy of waste is a subject which entails all aspects of society, including the elder care and the institution that are involved with this endeavor. The government pays the elderly as they are sick and unable to work through Medicare. Now this has created an economy for lots of people which involves taking care of the elderly people. For instance, medical professionals, such as nurses, medical assistants, LVNs, are there to aid these patients and care for their well beings and medical needs. However, when these professionals are used to care for an elderly per patients who is terminally ill and is just kept alive artificially by the help of technology, then the amount of waste created with the use of the facility of the hospital and payments used for the professionals and the number of drugs and highly expensive medications are wasted to keep these terminally ill patients for a few days and few months. This could be avoided if we let God and nature take its course and let the patient have the dignity of being with their family in their last days of living instead of being highly medicated and attached to many medical devices, which creates unnatural death scene and creates a spasm between God and the patient to leave this earthly world and die in peace. Another aspect of the elder care and having caretakers to come to one's home to take care of the elderly people in the house. Now although, this is a novice, it is a good thing to do however, people take advantage of this situation, both the caretaker and the elderly. Lots of the elderly people pretend to need assistance, where they are full capable of fending for themselves. Lots of the money goes to the same members of the family, therefore, creating income for the family, which is not legit or ethical if the elderly is healthy and is capable of taking care him or herself, why should you abuse the system just to get extra money for themselves or their family member. The system is there to help elderly people who are incapable of taking care of themselves and the government has created laws to help these people by hiring caretakers to be with these people in their home setting and taking care of them and their needs which is a good thing. But when the caretaker and the family members who act as caretakers take advantage of the laws and use the money for their own use or giving portions to the family members not because the family is unable but just for the extra money is not right. This creates wasted economy from the government when people abuse the government to create their own economy and increase their living standards. Those people are the type that lack ethics and family pride. It used to be that the family would take care of themselves till the older family member would die. However, because of the economy condition, which everybody works to make ends meet and you do not have family members staying home, therefore government created caretaker positions for eligible people, and was not intended for charitable purposes.

Another version of this economy of waste is at hospices and convalescent homes, although those institutions have been created to assist the patients and the terminally ill, either to regain their health or keep them comfortable in their last moments, but the abuse has been tremendous, done by the institutions themselves by the very caretakers themselves and by the insurance and medical companies. Medical companies sell billions of medications to those facilities and those facilities in return would keep these terminally ill people alive and breathing as long as possible by the help of very expensive medications or purely by keeping them sedated therefore extending their stay time in the facility so that the facility can make more profits from having those patients admitted. Ethically speaking, a dying person, in his last days should die with dignity, in his own home, surrounded by loving family members. Not to be sedated and die in state of being dazed and confused due to being highly medicated, in an unfamiliar facility surrounded by medical personnel. We know by technology and expense of millions of dollars there are drugs and there is machinery to keep some patients alive for days and months. Although, this is good and useful for the general public, youth and the working class, but when it comes to the terminally ill, it has become a wasteful endeavor to keep a dying patient just alive for the purpose of being alive just to make money off of this patient without too much care in his holistic care or situation, which does not make sense in another person perspective looking in from the outside. This is not what God intended for the dying person, to die in an unnatural setting.

22. The Economy of Waste: First Responders and Emergency

Another aspect of this economy of waste includes our emergencies and the way we carry things to the max. for any 911 phone calls that go through for needed medical help due to some protocols first responders always travel together, with the paramedics and the fire departments, which is many cases, the fire department should be excluded from situation. Most of the time, when the emergency calls are made, the situation is clearly explained to the dispatcher and most of the time it is clear the victim does not need assistance from the fire department and at times callers state they do not need the fire department yet the because of protocols and fear of being sued by patients, they go along for the ride anyways. When the fire department gets involved, it becomes much costlier for the city and sometimes for the patient. The better situation will be that the paramedics should rush to the scene but while they are driving, they can assess the need for the fire department to join or not. Another version would be, why not have highly skilled small attachments that they can ride with the paramedics to create solutions for unforeseen events they will always have some tools such as crowbars and hammers or any tool that can assist instead of having 10 men a truck to follow the paramedics for when one fireman can just tag along with the paramedics. Most of these cases arise not because of the need but because of the fear of getting sued from the patient. This is what is costly and there is no reason to have this situation.

Fire trucks and firefighters are used for extinguishing the accidental fires around the houses and wildfires. Sometimes, those firefighters do a great job and they get to the place on time and they do a great job to extinguish the fire but in other cases which we see a lot of, is, without really planning and really having the knowledge and assessments needed to tackle the problem, firefighters go into the job and some of them let the fire go and become bystanders or the bureaucracy at such that a small fire will not extinguished by the few firemen but they will wait for the captains orders on what to do. In those cases, those small fires become larger and larger and we eventually are faced with fires that are burn acres and acres of land uncontrollably. Furthermore, most of the time, when spoken with the firefighters, when it comes to the hills around the town, the question asked is "why don't they extinguish the fires with all force before it spreads uncontrollably causing so much damage" and their response is usually "it is good to get rid of the brush now so it will not burn later on." This response is so unthoughtful and simplistic because they do not comprehend the amount of damage they are creating for the environment and all the animal species that inhabit these areas along with the loss of acres of trees and greenery which create a balanced atmosphere and produce rain and oxygen for our environment. By letting those hills burn, they help the drought, they help with the polluted air and for years to come we do not have vegetations or animal groups to naturally sustain our environments and create moisture for rain and clear air. We all clap and appreciate what a good job fire fighter are doing but, these fires can be controlled majority of the time instead of neglected. There should be a real study done and investigations to really understand how to control these fires, how to put them out and what effects they have on the environment at large. To control these wildfires, especially in California, there are many solutions, such as creating artificial lakes, wherever possible in close distances of the mountains, so when a fire does arise, the water can be used nearby instead of making the trip further to collect more water. Those manmade lakes will make the environment much more beautiful and people can enjoy these beautiful lakes and it will create enough moisture for additional rains and enhance firefighting when needed. The other option would be creating separation roadways between the acreages with water pipes installed so in the time of fire, firemen, can easily get a hold of the needed water though these pipes and the roadway itself should be wide enough that it would stop fires from jumping and spreading from one acre to the other. Additionally, those fire roads can be helped by installing prefab tall railings which can be done with the firefighters just before the fire reaches the next area and it will avoid any spreading of the fire. Those are a few thoughts about the wasted money and environmental hazards that have been created. We are sure that with the research and real concern about those fires, much better methods can be found which will make our dollars instead of creating droughts, use it for the stopping of fires and keeping our environment clean.

23. The Economy of Waste: Medicine

This is a real problem in our society. The drug makers with their huge budget, with their economic clout have created havoc on people and forcing doctors to use their drugs knowing that those drugs are although safe but either they are useless or has minimum effect on the patient. This way the drug makers sells tones of drugs worldwide, by making people to use exceptionally low dosage of the drug so they can prolong the use of the medicine and pay arm and leg for it. Also, in this conspiracy the insurance companies have lots of say that drug makers and insurance companies make every single patient user of their medicine and insurance payers. Therefore, patients, patiently take those medicines which doctors have prescribed for them, bunch of that everyday few times. So, this abuse of medicine usage creates long term effect and other side effects that needs to be treated with another bunch of medicines proscribe by doctors and produced by this mega-drug makers. In fact, most of those sicknesses could be cured by time or use of more potent medicine for a short while with accurate dosages for treatment. It is funny and absurd to check the medicine cabinets of people with so many drugs that one thinks, are they for sale or are they crazy to take so many medicines few times a day?! The waste of economy on abuse of those drug is huge on that people spend their hard-earned money on drugs or on insurance companies to provide those drugs for them. On the other hand, this phenomenon creates huge employment and work for thousands of people.

24. Economy of Waste: Drugs legal/illegal

In our society, the use and abuse of drugs whether legal or illegal, is in such a huge quantity that the price paid for it in dollar amount, and health or death of people is unimaginable and reaches in billions of dollars. The waste in people's life and amount of money spent on buying those legal/illegal drugs is such a tremendous amount that creates both economy and waste of economy in our society. The drug use is in such a way that causes death of many people and make lots of others sick such that either they are hospitalized, they are homeless or are disabled to be working men and women in the society with only need of others to provide and take care of them.

Because of their sickness, those drug users create havoc on economy and government agencies and hospitalization costs for people and insurance companies. Some of those drug users, end up either in streets as homeless or they do felony acts which end up engaging police force and filling the jails, costing millions of dollars for government and taxpayers. The legalized weed producers and sellers although create some economy but mostly few owners make millions of dollars in cash without paying any taxes. On the other hand, the poor users because of the addiction spends millions of dollars on these illegal drugs and break up their family, do felony acts, involve in costly accidents or become homeless which is huge cost for cities and heath organizations. Government spend taxpayer's money to provide homes and other services for those homeless but because of their abuse the number of those homelessness grows, and governments are not capable to keep up with their demands and increase in their numbers every day. Another huge cost to society due to this drug use and abuse is the breakdown of the families which costs billions in servicing those families economically and the mental damage that those broken families and going through. Most of the times, kids in these families end up getting supported by governments either as childcare support or they end up in foster cares which is prelude to life of loneliness anger and eventually becoming the drug users themselves. Mothers in those broken families, with lots of heartache and trauma, try to put together their lives, and start another life with another person which this creates lots of pain for the kids. Also, losing of the income and home is another burden and expense they have to deal with for a long time which most of the time they end up with not being able to pay the mortgages or rents and become homeless themselves because of the family breakdown.

25. The Economy of Waste: Vitamins

In recent decades, the use of vitamins has been in such an increase that has created another wasted economy by people and their families paying their hard-earned money on buying vitamins which their benefits are under question and on the top of it they pay heavy price for advertised and brand-named vitamins. Although, some of those vitamins may provide some benefits but since it becomes daily fashion, not taking of those vitamins makes you a less of man or woman in the society. The vitamin makers collect billions of dollars out of those products by heavy advertising in different kinds of media and they lure people to buy and use those vitamins because for example if not their skin will not shine, their hair will not be as strong, their health will diminish, they will lose their muscularity, or their body will not in shape as it must be. Therefore, the vitamin use and abuse has reach in such a level that whole new industry is created in the world without having exact benefit level determined by professionals because most of those vitamins are over the counter and none of the doctors or professionals have really tested their activeness or benefit level. People use those items really by their peers advertising or they have seen or heard the heavy advertising in social media by those vitamin producing companies. As it is obvious the economy of waste in this vitamin usage, when people spend so much money for items not of their needs but advised by advertising companies who are paid by those producing companies with the goal of making huge profits.

26. The Economy of Waste: Organic Products

The organic products are the other fads that in recent years have become popular with sellers and consumers. Sellers of those supposedly organic products have hipped the price of almost the same material by calling it organic and make a huge profit out of backs of families, mothers and fathers who so much care for their family members that they are willing to spend much more of their hard-earned money on organic products because it surpassingly is healthier and have better quality. The distinction between those farm products of organic and non-organic are so minute that the hype created by big advertising companies and businesses made almost universal to use the high-priced organic verses the normal farm products used for ages. The economy of waste is so apparent in this matter that clever businessmen by naming their products as organic they are making thousands of profits. In reality, changing of the way the farm is done by adding or subtracting some enhancers and fertilizers and reduction or change in use of pesticides they claim that they have achieved organic product verses the common way of producing those materials from the natures. This slight changes in production methodology really does not have any additional cost to produce the material but only because of the name Organic they branded it; they are selling the same product with a much higher price. It is such an irony, that naturally produced items which was consumed for ages, first, they added some fertilizers and pesticides to increase the production amount then, produced the same natural materials with additional certain gins to alter its quality and increase the production and now by changing the fertilizers and pesticides amounts they are calling it organic and selling it that way to make big profit out of those changes.

PART IV

SYSTEMS

27. The Economy of Waste: Legal System

At the time of the Prophet Moses, there was probably no written laws therefore, he was the first one who came up with the 10 commandments inspired by God. Since then, countries have created more laws to cover all aspects of conduct between governments, between people, between cities, counties and conduct of people in that certain city under cities required laws. Those lawbooks have increased tremendously every year. Some countries have limits to the laws created and the laws are general in nature and the judges make the interpretation for that case. However, in the US, particularly, due to the judicial system and its concepts, the laws have multiplied daily because it is not only coming from the judges but from the lawyers themselves, they advocate those additional laws, that eventually find a way for the legal system. Furthermore, the legal system has become so thick and cumbersome that no ordinary people can relate or understand what the law entails. This creates an opportune time for the lawyers to use this hidden treasure for their benefits and conning or rightfully getting paid millions of dollars by the common people so that they can defend them. Because of this situation, becoming a lawyer, is very profitable in our society and our youth, rather than becoming doctors, engineers, architects, they go for law school because of the major profits and selfish beneficial reasons and all the hype and status that some of the lawyers receive because of this scandalous and rich clientele paying millions so that they can get away with murder in the presence of media and the drama created by networks and other social media outlets. Now let us look at this in the sense of economy of waste. Due to this demand for lawyers to understand the laws and supposedly protect us from lawsuits and begin wrongfully accused or protect us from judgement although we have done something wrong and some of the rich, they pay millions and they get away with murder, rape, fraud, embezzlement in their businesses or life, etc. This economy, which is created by tremendous amounts of laws and lawyers, although creates lots of jobs for common people, like paralegals, assistants, medical groups that assist the lawyers and their work, all of this creates lots of jobs, which is good for some ordinary people and society however, simultaneously, this wasted economy creates lots of heartache, lots of disappointment, lots of suicide, depression and anxieties, tremendous amount of divorce. Basically, we are tearing the fabric of society, the innocence of society, the morality of family structures, ethics of people and the cities and the nation. Some victorious individuals who have avoided judgement or some innocent people that cleared their names by these lawyers, they appreciate the system but there are tremendous amounts of people who get annoyed and taken advantage, harassed, and pay lots of money just to keep their heads above the water for the futile lawsuits. In our judgement, having a system which has element of ethics in it and tries to help and preserve people's innocence by not only using man made laws but having God in their minds and being open for common people to understand what the laws are about. The laws should be specific, result oriented, not full of bylaws which makes things harder to understand. These by laws should not entail writings full fine print and should cut to the chase quickly without being written for lawyers only and shouldn't be full of hundreds of pages to thousands, whereas the average Joe does not speak contract laws and will never understand what they are agreeing to unless a paid professional lawyer is present and most of the time the average

Joe will not have that assistance, therefore causing a trap for a common person with misrepresentation and misleading facts without prior knowledge to the information at hand. Why should laws be written that a common man, a God-fearing man cannot comprehend so he can apply those laws in his daily life. We are not advocating ten commandments only but, we are saying there should be a limit to number of laws that we create and make the laws only for the lawyers to understand and the people become the pawn for the lawyers which makes it easier to con these average civilians. There should be more clear stated contracts that people can abide by and understand so it does not create any confusion. Economy has grown by this unethical lawsuit, which has no outcome but to con money from one to another and lawyers' profit from this whole interaction.

Another portion of this economy of waste through the legal system is getting help from another aspect of society, which is merely the healthcare and the health professionals and doctors, there is a triangle in the legal system consist of the petitioner, the attorneys and the doctor, involved in that certain situation, for instance in an accident, which could be resolved very amicably between both parties or insurance company ends up in the hands of the lawyer who persuades the client to immediately seek a doctors help or health institution to create a lawsuit based on pain, suffering or maybe actual physical damage. Those sufferings in the physical damages are exaggerated by the doctors who have connections with the lawyers sometimes just to make the case more profitable and worthier of large settlements, which in reality this whole thing can be finished with only percentage of the cost they went through. This example, although created jobs for the layers, jobs of the doctors and their assistants, but it wasted the precious money of the economy.

28. The Economy of Waste: Traffic system

In economy of the waste, the traffic and the waste associated with it is such a tremendous amount that almost every aspect of the life in capitalist system is somehow related. Beside money wasted on luxury cars there are items such as the type of gasoline used, freeway construction with lots of maintenance cost, bridges, and additional lines just for once in a great moon accident. Due to lack of public transportation which is created by bureaucracies and big capital the freeways, roads and streets are filled with many types of cars and other transportation means so creating the biggest waste of all by cars lining in jammed traffics, wasting billions gallon of gas, wasting people's time waiting in traffic to clear, accidents happening so often, the injured and faulty low suits due to accidents, all these together create both the economy and huge waste that could easily be avoided. Traffic, besides having physical, mental and wasted labor time, associated cost has another facet which is the environment and the pollution in air that causes many illnesses for people.

One might ask in the name of economy and progress what a waste we are creating by having all those cars in streets, roads, and freeways. This is wasted economy since one could easily create public transportation such as buses, metro, taxi, trains and bicycle lanes which will reduce the traffic, pollution, wasted time of people in traffic and the cost associated with maintenance of the cars, insurances paid for cars, and the payments for leasing or buying cars. One can see that those billions of cars on the road, although create huge economy for the country and the people to work but in the hide side, it creates such a tremendous waste for environment, thousands of people dying in accidents, hospitals full of injured people from accidents and getting sick because of air pollution caused by traffic. All these wastes can be controlled by thinking in humane way of life. In an utopian lifestyle, all we need is a good system of transportation that should be pollution free by use of battery or electric system not producing air pollution and traffic. Also, by having driverless cars in the near future, not everybody needs cars in their garages with that wasted costs that all they need is to call a driverless car to pick them up and go wherever they need to. Money saved with these futuristic systems the government and especially big companies will save millions and they will be obliged to give back to the society their fair share of that profits so many jobless people and the poor can receive salaries so they can live a normal life.

29. The Economy of Waste: Fires

Fires are another natural disaster that causes huge devastation, destroys lives, burns thousands of acres of brush and trees, pollutes the air, which causes lots of sickness and hospital bills. The wasted economy on this fire scenarios are that the governments spend lots of money for those firefighters to get paid and wait for a natural calamity such as those large fires in California to burn and create a havoc on people and environment, few times a year. Although, we appreciate all those firefighters in time of fire and other emergencies, but realistically they are getting highly paid with union wages, for yearlong employment and overtime pay for few hours in a day or week possible work. Rather than those firefighters be used only part time but being paid full time for their services, it would be much more desirable that those firefighters with proper education and knowhow in forestry they can manage and maintain the whole hillside and brush areas in such a manner that is humanly possible to extinguish any fire in very short time. They need to learn how to divide, create roads and facilities in between the land parcels, to deforest or forest where needed, build fences and infrastructures for water delivery, for expected fires. For example, in Europe some countries have more brush and trees than in California, but they manage so professionally that the firs are at minimum and whenever it happens, they put the fire down in a shot timing, so the fire does not create havoc on people and environment. Due to lack of proper education, and knowing the environment and ways of preventing fires or if it stats to eliminated as soon as possible those firefighters sadly think that the best solution is to let the hillside to burn with all its destruction and loss of life loss of buildings and pollution of the air and so on thinking that this solution is better than surpassingly very, costly, other solutions, and their conclusion is since the hillside is burned this year they will not have that fire situation for coming year because everything is burned. This mentality is very wrong because by burning the whole hillside with many acres of land they destroy not only trees and brushes which produces oxygen and is part of sustaining of the nature but also all the specious including birds, mouse, and other animals are either killed or relocated from that area disturbing the natural harmony of that area, and the pollution in air which lingers in air for months and people breathing those polluted airs are getting sick, therefore, they need to use hospitals, doctors, medicine to get better meanwhile spending lots of hard-earned money for this situation. With proper education of those firefighters, we could save millions of wasted funds on devastation, firefighting, and rebuilding.

30. The Economy of Waste: Homelessness

In the United States of America, the phenomena of homelessness have increased manifold and hundreds of thousands of fellow citizens including men, women and children are homeless in large cities. This situation is incredibly sad and costly issue for the cities, environment and people living in cities creates cost for hospital care and help spreading many diseases. The government and the people spend millions of dollars to try helping that homelessness by providing shelters, building housing units in the middle of downtown which is very costly. The other cost involve with this homelessness is the huge cost they bring about by being sick all the time and using emergency hospitalization, which costs millions of dollars for hospitals. The cities pass ordinances and laws to tax people for the homelessness by increasing the property taxes or other taxes to help that homelessness but unfortunately due to government's bureaucracy, and inefficiency in implementing those budgets properly, the waste is tremendous, and the results are minute. Those obscured amount of waste both in dollar amount and lives lost is a good example of "Economy of Waste" which people and government spend and waste their money to help those homeless people. Without bureaucracy and fruitless lawsuits brought by many hungry lawyers regarding the rights of those homeless people, they create a havoc on society and homeless themselves. The homeless situation could be solved very amicably by use of sound judgment, engineering knowhow and practical solutions. To provide remedy for the situation, first, there should be a good study done of the type, reasons, and nature of homelessness. Those who are sick either mentally or physically need to be differentiated and sent to proper clinics or hospitals for treatment, those mentally disturb persons should be sent to proper institutions for long time treatment and rehabilitations. Those homeless people which are drug addicted, should be sent to rehab centers for recovery. The government or businesses should build small temporary housing units in less populated and cheaper areas away from downtown and possibly in countryside.

Those temporary structures should be surrounded with parks, clinics, rehab centers, exercise areas and warehouses with job trainings and education centers for both youth and elder. Those centers would be an ideal place to help those families and individuals who are out of work and means of survival to take a break, educate and train themselves for new jobs and mentally get help to survive on their own. Those facilities will have trained tutors, doctors, educators, entrepreneurs, and consultants to teach those homeless to rebuild their life and learn new means of survival. Those centers will be much cheaper to construct and run when they are in countryside not units build in downtown which is ten times more expensive and does not have all the facilities mentioned above. There is always some criticism that by moving those people to city perimeters, one infringes on the rights of those homeless to stay wherever they want specially in downtown. But the solution is easy to have a bus system to take those who would like to travel to downtown or some other places on daily bases. Therefore, by using those pragmatic solutions, we will eliminate the heartache, diseases, the humility caused by homelessness and people becoming shameful by seeing those homeless people in the filth living in their neighborhood.

In America, with its all strength and wealth, it is travesty and shameful to have homeless living in those pitiful conditions. Many countries, which are much poor situation or smaller with less wealth, they do not have these homeless issues. Usually, on those countries, families and relatives are taking care of the needy and sick member of their family or the government take very sick or mentally disturbed people to the proper institutions not letting them to live in streets on their own.

31. The Economy of Waste – No bus or Taxi

To create the most waste possible way, they got rid of any transportation that will facilitate your life and reduce the headache in transportation. For instance, if a bus can take 50 people from A to B just observe amount of waste, if you would create by acquiring 50 cars instead, let us look at it: Traffic jam created by too many cars in roads, reduce speed, use of at least 20 times more fuel than a single bus, more accident, more break down, more smog checks for cars, more car services, mechanic shop, gas station, body shops and etc. With this one small example we can see how this "waste" will create thousands of jobs, put more burden on people to work harder just to pay for this car's repairs and thousands of accidents, waste fuels etc. Darn thing about it, is that we all are happy to have the so calling luxury of owning their car to go from A to B, no matter the cost of payment and upkeep and spend more of our precious time just to drive a car. We pay but we are happy, and everybody is working is not this heaven!!!

These darn slave drivers and slave keepers with this slave work with little food and big amount of resistances and exceedingly small output from their slaves, probably would benefit tremendously, with today's waste mentality, instead of chains and hunger of slaves, they would have bought a car for those slaves who would go to work much faster, work harder and have a huge output and to be proud for being owner of that nice brand new car…no complaining, no resisting to slave owners, always ready to work, and to hope that one day they will be able to buy a car and go to work by themselves.

32. The Economy of Waste: Wars

Wars are another excellent example of "Economy of Waste." Governments spend billions of dollars every year in acquiring, creating, designing, and building highly sophisticated weaponry, prepare themselves for future wars. This act, which takes big bite out of the country's budget, although necessary for safety of the country and it produces huge amounts of employment for people but at the same time, because of the system, there are lots of waste in producing those weaponry and some of those weapons are so advance that takes billions to get the task accomplished. Governments in some ways, if they spend all those billions of dollars in more education and improving their relationship with their neighbors so they do not need to get into expensive wars every few years. This way, countries can save all those billions of dollars and spend on wellbeing of people and construct infra structures, roads, and other necessary institutions. on the other hand, when a war starts, the destructions brought about by bombings and other means of conducting war is so huge for both waring parts that in matter of few days, they cost of the destruction reaches to billions of dollars and it takes years to reconstruct the housing, buildings, institutions, roads and infrastructures, facilities, airports, airplanes and so on. Those billions of dollars spend on these wars and including the tragedy of soldiers and people being killed is a travesty. All those wastes of human beings, buildings and cities and roads, which is totally waste, minus the gratifications of egos of some people such as presidents of rulers in some countries wanting more and more to self-gratify or to show his power and zeal to carry those huge destruction and heart ache to the neighboring countries. People like Hitler have caused the humility and nations of billions and billions of dollars of expense in destruction and millions of lives lost because of his stupid ambition of running the word by himself. All those wasted lives and distractions in one hand if could have been avoided, would have saved millions of lives and billions of hard-earned monies for countries. The agencies such as united nations or even the governments of countries themselves, if spend only portion of that waste to better understand the world and their neighbors needs and come up with a pragmatic solution for the situations arrived, then there would not be any wars with wasting billions of dollars.

Sarcastically speaking, after wars are finished, all that destructions is an opportunity for countries to spend billions to reconstruct all the damaged infrastructures, roads, buildings, institutions, schools, and hospitals. This endure creates lots of jobs for people and a good possibility to rebuild the ruined old buildings by new and modern ones instead. Therefore, we can see that through all that waste there is a blooming of new economy and work for people gone through those stupid wars. In twenty first century, it is sad to see there are still wars happening and lives getting effected and economy and livelihood of people are getting wasted by these wars. Instead, the countries if spent those wasted money on studying themselves and their neighbors, try to accommodate each other, educate their people and change their politics, think each one are a member of the same body that way if any part is hurt it will affect all other parts too. The world bodies such as united nation, ones for all should finalized the boundaries of each country, so there are no more wars about the size of a country or expansion of it. Secondly, those world bodies should think of world government and come up with solutions for the needs, aspirations, industrial help, humanitarian help in time to pandemics and natural disasters so the countries could get over all the calamities and deviation brought by above mentioned situations. We all are united on this planet and we should all think not only for ourselves but for others wherever they are. This mentality will help for future generations not to get into wars and waste lots of money and lives but survive and be prosperous against all those naturals and human made devastations.

PART V
POLITICES

33. The Economy of Waste: Communism

Economy of waste or lack of it, is also vividly shown in communism, in the countries ruled by communist propaganda. Although, those communist countries provided free housing, jobs, vacations, transportation, education, art, sport, etc. which all are great for a society to live in comfortable life but in lieu of all those free services provided by government, the absence of the economy of waste, caused the downfall of many communist countries. On those countries although people had houses, there were no luxury items to show off and enjoy. There were not too many luxury goods besides the essential living items. There was free transportation so there was no reason to mass produce different cars with different brands and colors, so people buy and sell to help the economy of the country and pay taxes on it. Jobs were provided for people, so they did not have to compete for getting jobs or creating new projects and making profit of those new jobs. At the same time arts and sports were highly appreciated and the athletics were worldwide famous but due to lack of economy of waste those games and arts were free so, there were no competition, no athletic clubs to make billions every year, no high end or brand name goods and products to sell to customers and make a good money out of it. In the other hand, there were lots of waste in human working hours, workers got into the factory wasted their eight hours or more by producing extraordinarily little which could have been produced in an hour in other non-communist countries. Also, because of lack of enough equipment and goods and waste in time in factories, people start stealing from the factories where they were working, or they just did not go to work but an associate filled their timecard. As we can see, due to lack of waste the economy of those communist countries went down and eventually the whole system was removed under the pressure of lack of economy progress and those countries joined the free world to use economy of waste to enhance their economy and wealth. Those communist countries failed to understand the "Economy of Waste" and its benefits in improving the economy of the country and the happiness of its people who were dreaming to have the cloths, jewelries, cars and other household items of the luxuries of non-communist countries. On the other hand, due to workers not having competition or gaining rewards in their job sites they wasted the time by producing minimum goods and down grading the country's economy.

Communists should create competition and variety of goods for people to enjoy and not to steal. They should open up the heavy government rules and let people to decide some of the aspects of life and work, let them have their own companies and the businesses and be free in some ways to produce their own or create their own businesses. This way although the government does the majority of the work, but people have some say on their livelihood and because of this freedom and competition people will enjoy more of the new goods and services which intern will reduce their dissatisfaction with government or they will eliminate the wasted hours in their factories and use their free hours to work for themselves and make more habitable and enjoyable society. The "Economy of Waste" is a tool to cherish but not to abuse it. It is a gift that governments by providing sensible laws and limits on the abuse of it can encourage and help people to live both in competition and comfort at the same time. This way, the balance in use of this theory will provide a healthier, happier society.

34. The Economy of Waste: Capitalism

In capitalist countries, in opposed to communist countries wasting too much ruins the life of people. Everybody is in race to jump ahead of "Joneses" and in this process they waste a life of tranquility, time with friends and family, time to enjoy or not to do anything. In capitalism countries, rest is gone! Everyone is working more and more hours, using theories like 10X to do more projects in less of a time as possible, multi tasks, make more money, waste more money on un-needed goods, get new housings and businesses, try to run those companies efficiently, worry about all of them every night, worry about how to save the money or how to spend on stock market, which market to pick to make more money or spend sleepless nights worrying about stock that they lost. Families really are not families anymore because lack of time and doing too many jobs everybody is for themselves, they want to be the next milliner. Therefore, mom and dads are working, kids over 16 are working besides going to school. Kids are sent to daycares or babysitters are taking care of them in lieu of mom or dad. The "Economy of Waste" has gone too far and been abused by people and institutions to work hard, make more money and waste more and in this way they lost their peace of mind and the real meaning of their life. Therefore, use of this weapon, meaning the "Economy of Waste" should be really studied and put a limit in its uses or abuse of it. Countries should encourage a middle ground in using this weapon and not encourage their people to go war with this weapon for the purpose of killing only not knowing WHY? Politicians, historians and philosophers they all have to study this subject and produce a simple guideline for people to learn not to abuse this weapon, and governments should create rules to implement those guidelines and encourage people to work and live in a healthier manner. Capitalist can reduce their demands on working people, encourage healthy living, reduce the work hours, reduce the desire to compete with "Joneses," use moderation in acquiring and wasting things, limit the wants and try to live in a state of happiness with natural surroundings rather than unneeded luxury items, and unhealthy competition with neighbors.

35. The Economy of Waste: "Educated" Socialism

There are many socialistic countries in the world specially in Europe. In a socialistic system the government tries to take care of people and their health issues mainly for the additional taxes they collect. This way, poor people under certain income level are protected and given enough support by government to live in a rather safe and livable condition. In theory after the certain limit people can earn whatever they can with their businesses and other sources only by paying the required taxes which is higher percentage for higher earners, this way the wealth is distributed to the people themselves not letting rich people to keep most of the money. In such a system, rich individuals can not compete with the rich people in a capitalism system who pay much lower taxes, are much powerful and have more investment power to create new businesses and make much more profit. In an "Educated Socialism" the concept we introduce is to have a true socialistic system with 21st century knowhow and government and all its agencies try their best to help and bring together the lower earning people first to have a middle-class living standard and secondly, they work on their lifestyle and should have training in music, athletics, education and better human relationship.

In a communist country the emphasis was put on the same lifestyle which produced great athletes in all fields and great musicians, arts and theater, writers, philosophers and so on. Therefore, by having an educated "Socialism System" the economy of the waste should be moderated in such a way that the hype in capitalism system is removed and the minimum standards of "Economy of Waste" is improved to manageable and healthy levels. This way, people whether rich or poor, can have a very descent standard of living and they are not enticed so much to sacrifice their life and family for uphill of capitalistic living. In future due to great progress in Robotics where robots are doing most of the work, and cars are driven by them and most of the industrial work including warehouse managements and others are taking cared by itself therefore there would be not enough working place or work for people and unemployment will be huge, that is the reason we need this new educated socialism to balance the lifestyle of the people and provide a humane and adequate living standards for all the people regardless of their income.

36. The Economy of Waste: Conclusion

I have started to write this book about 15 years ago and during years, I have personally experienced most of the items written in this booklet. Although, the headings and items mentioned are common sense and ordinary, but it is the economy of our country in a nutshell. The 'Economy of waste," is a double-edged sword, it is both good and bad at the same time. This "Economy of Waste," in one hand, it waste lots of goods and manpower, brings down the earnings of the families which they have to spend extra on the hyped items and unnecessary expenses, un-wanted items, items bought based on the wants and not based on the needs, lots of time wasted to do unnecessary appointments, staying in traffic, vacationing in highly expensive hotels regardless of its cost for the family, marching with "Joneses," enjoying the good life, forgetting our slave mentality of hard work, sleepless nights, worry about all those projects that needs to be done in that time frame, all and all are to catch up with "Joneses" and to be a good citizen in this industrial country with plenty of work... so much work but not enough time to get it done, cut sleep time to just a few hours per day, drinking high energy drinks, having few cups of coffee, running like dogs in this crazy fulfillment, busy life style, making more money, spend it as if there is no tomorrow, we are young, healthy, we have vitamins taken, all the lab work and MRI done for the conceivable future sicknesses, we had all appointments filled for face lift and meeting the fitness guru. No wonder worldwide people are dreaming to come to this country and be part of this paradise living with its lights, expensive cars and luxurious homes, Los Vegas to spend tons of money and have honeymoon in Hawaii. All they have to do is to be part of this herd of employees and intrapreneurs going through the life with gusto and determination to make it, no matter what sacrifices they make to themselves, to their family and society, because they are too busy to think about those matters, Dollar is the King and they are all rushing and pushing their way to get it, no matter how much of waste they make or how many lives they destroy on the way...

In pursuit of this heaven, people from all over the world try to get to the place by any means and ways they can, sometimes walking across the desert with their families some children dies, but they survive to get to their place, others get their boats, overloaded with immigrants and dreamers, some succeed others sunk in the ocean, other families wait for months or years at immigration stations, waiting for mighty green cards, some losing their family members, kids or elders in the minimum facility stations. All and all immigrants will do anything and pay lots of money upfronts to bunch of thieves and human traffickers to take them or their family members to the promised land. Those lucky immigrants who succeed to enter the country, they have to work extremely hard to be able to survive in this unknown community with no English knowledge, learn the language and regulations including traffic, insurance, taxation, accounting and credit rules. Those new commers waste ten to fifteen years of their life to learn the new system and then since they have already accustomed to the system, they work harder, sleepless to catch up with neighbors to have multiple cars, new house, vacations etc. Now this seasoned immigrant is in condition to rule the world and be the epidemy of rich and famous, be part of the meaning of heaven, be the one to look for and strive for his achievement. This burning economy has created many jobs for employees to work. That is the reason unemployment is down to single digits, everyone is working, even in some areas there are not enough workers to be employed that is the reason, governments and some other institutions actively seek employees whether educated or not, from other countries. This phenomenon is great and useful for country, because all these workers who work, pay taxes, and have money to spend on goods and they are helping the economy. The government with the huge amount of taxes gained are engaging in buildings roads, schools, and institutions. The army gets big chunk of government money to get bigger, bolder and have the latest and greatest machinery and airlines, guns and submarines, to show the world that they are the most power full and number one in the world. The government with this new gained power start pushing other countries and governments to give concessions and sell their products much cheaper than they should have. Due to the huge economy other countries take a note of it and try to sell their goods and natural resources to this reach country. Therefore, those countries become so dependent to the reach countries that they lose their independence and their economy and lifestyle always are affected by the polices and requirements of the rich countries.

All these hype and hard work, waste and Economy creates another side of the "Economy of Waste," which shines through the double edge sward. Due to huge economy and the waste created by that in all aspects of its expansion, those waste have tremendous effect on environment and on people's life.

The environment is polluted with trash in lands and seas, by killing thousands of specious of animals and fishes which were part of the nature. Besides, the environment, the huge production of oil and gases specially, methane and other harmful ones, have created a havoc on our breathing air causing many sicknesses and diseases, and most importantly creating the climate warming which in itself has melted north pole snows, causing catastrophic tornadoes, and huge multi-acres of burning fires. Just look at California which skies are full of smoke, hard to breath and check the huge tornadoes in coast of Texas and Florida. Another aspect of this Economy of Waste is due to empathy between rich and poor countries and dependence of poor countries who may have natural resources only, they suffered tremendously because they do not peruse an independent economy, but they become enslave to the huge requirement of rich countries and their requirement and theories. Another side of this is the brain drain of those poor countries which is the young educated, smart doctors, businessmen, inventers, they all to be the greedy human beings and wanting the best life for themselves and their families so they try to immigrate to those rich countries to build their future. It is also helpful for them to be part of lottery system of gaining green cards to move to the rich country.

In other look, those poor countries despite some of them having huge amounts of natural resources are poor and backward as it commonly called third world countries. The biggest mistakes of those countries are not knowing the "Economy of Waste." They are not aware of possibilities and economic gains, employment and good life associated with this phenomenon. People live in their homes which have been built with their grand grandfathers for generations without doing much of remodeling, renovation, or additions. So, they lose the huge economy associated with spending money, buying materials, getting workers to work, and having better housing. Another big issue is that those old houses which have paid off for many years do not create any economy because nobody gets a loan to do other work, open new businesses with that money or there are no institutions such as banks to provide them with loans with interests that in itself create huge economy and employment for those who are working for them. Due to those accumulated interests, the banks and other institutions can invest and create more work and economy for the country. Because of lack of competition, and walking with "Joneses," there is no reason for people to change their way of life. That is why they stay the same with no new changes, new clothing, new cars, new furniture, asphalting the dirt roads or bringing electricity to villages, having clean water, having new machinery for farming. Therefore, everything is old, and things are done the way it was done ages ago. No progress, no hypes, no economy of waste and no luxury houses, no high-rises, no big institutions, etc.

ABOUT THE AUTHOR

Oksen Babakhanian, an accomplished structural engineer who owned his consulting structural engineering business for more thirty years. He has recently started writing few mini books after sale of his business perusing his childhood dream of being a writer. His booklets are mostly about his experiences and world knowledge. As an engineer, he tries to enhance the social and economic situation of the society both in home and abroad. His topics includes Rebirth of Cultural and Business Revolution in Armenia, Social Standing of African American People, Robotics and Educated Socialism System and The Economy of Waste.

Printed in the United States
by Baker & Taylor Publisher Services